LOST IN THE WOODS: A Children's Survival Guide

Copyright Lance Hodge, 2014
All rights reserved

ISBN **978-1503264922**

Printed in the United States of America

Color these trees!

Lost in the woods

A Children's Survival Guide

By Lance Hodge

Color these trees!

What would you do if you got lost in the woods?

Which way is the trail? I think I'm lost.

Would you hide behind a rock?

Or could you build a cabin and just live there?

Would you yell for help?

How would you stay warm at night?

What if a bear came by?

Would you hide?

Would you run?

Could you scare him away?

Ok, he's gone. Now what should I do?

Would you hike to a hill and look around?

And what would you eat?

Who would you talk to?

What if it rained?

Or snowed?

And how long would it take for somebody to find you?

And if you started walking, would you know which way to go?

But, if you got lost in the woods...

And you stayed right there...

It wouldn't be too long before somebody came looking.

And if you stayed
right there...

They would find you.

...and bring you home.

Color me!

Tell your friends what you've learned in this book!

Color this dog and these trees!

THE END

Color these trees!

Books to take along...

The Dream Writer, By Lance Hodge
ISBN-10: 1500616648   ISBN-13: 978-1500616649

Hannah's BIG Dream, By Lance Hodge
ISBN-10: 1500818720   ISBN-13: 978-1500818722

∞

A Paramedic's Guide: Wilderness First Aid, By Lance Hodge
ISBN-10: 1500182664   ISBN-13: 978-1500182663

 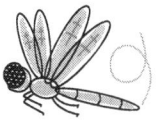

The first two books help to elevate vocabulary and teach children to enjoy discovering new words and learning new things.

The perfect books for parents to read along with their child and encourage inquisitiveness and the joy of reading.

Lance Hodge

PARENTS: Some things to talk about with your children

1. If you get lost you need to stop right where you are. If you keep walking, you'll go further and further away from where you should be; you'll get even more lost! So STOP, wait there, and somebody will find you.

2. You should call for help. Don't wear out your voice, but call out "HELP!" every few minutes. Somebody is already looking for you; you want them to hear you so they can find you. After you call for help, stop and listen, you might hear them calling back to you.

3. There's a chance they might not find you right away. It may get dark and you may have to spend the night outside. If that happens, be brave. It will be a little scary but remember the morning will come and the sun will come up.

4. If you have any extra clothes with you, put them *all* on if it's cold. If you have zippers and buttons on your clothes zip or button them up tight to keep warm. If you have a hat put in on. Try not to get wet, that will make you colder. Look for someplace to get out of the wind, next to a large rock or tree maybe. You might have to use leaves or pine needles to cover up with at night. You also want to make a bed to lay on out of leaves or pine needles to keep you off of the cold dirt.

5. If a bear or coyote or some sort of animal comes by you should try to scare them away, you can yell at them and act mean, and that should scare them away. Most animals in the forest can run faster than you can, so running away isn't usually a good idea. Try to scare them away. You can throw rocks or sticks at them while you yell at them to "Go away!"

6. If you can't stop right where you are for some reason you might want to go to a small hill or high place nearby, from there you might be able to see where you are and somebody might see you if they are looking for you from an airplane.

7. You don't have to eat right away; you will get hungry but you won't starve. But you DO need water right away. Find water that looks clean if you can and drink enough to feel full.

8. You should talk to yourself. Tell yourself somebody will find you soon, and remind yourself that everything is going to be OK. It's nice to talk, it scares away animals that hear you, and someone looking for you might hear you and find you easier, and it isn't quite as scary if you talk about how everything is going to be OK, and how you'll be home soon.

9. If it rains or snows you have to try to keep dry and warm. It's drier under big trees. You might find some sort of shelter from wind and rain around big rocks. Do your best to find a place that keeps you out of the rain or snow or wind; even if it's not a perfect place, it's better than no place. A fat tree might be the perfect place to block the wind.

10. If they don't find you today, they will probably find you tomorrow. Don't give up. Be brave. You have to be strong and smart. Animals can live outside and so can you. If you get really cold and start to shiver you can *dance*. Some people in really cold weather have danced for HOURS to keep themselves warm. Try not to get sweaty, don't dance too hard, remember you don't want to get wet, that makes you colder.

11. Remember, you don't know which way to go, that's how you got lost. But if you STOP right where you are it will be easier for people to find you, if you keep walking you will probably walk in the wrong direction, and that will get you more and more lost, and it will make it harder for people to find you. STAY WHERE YOU ARE. Stop right there and wait if you think you are lost. Stop walking! Wait right there!

12. Getting lost doesn't sound like fun. So, be careful NOT to get lost. Stay with your parents, stay close to camp, and don't go off by yourself. Always stay on the trail. If you lose

the trail and think you are lost, STOP WHERE YOU ARE. Call out for "HELP!" Someone will come soon and find you.

13. Keep this book in your backpack or day pack. If you ever go walking make sure you wear a day pack, bring water, a jacket, a hat, a space blanket, and a flashlight; also bring this book!

14. <u>You should have a loud whistle with you all the time</u>. Wear it around your neck *all the time* when you're on a camping trip. People can hear that whistle from far away, and it's better than yelling.

15. This book shouldn't scare you, it's meant to make you *think* about things that you should know. It's meant to make sure you are safe and that you are ready to help yourself if you do get lost. Knowing what to do makes you strong and smart, you become powerful! Now you know what to do if you get lost!

16. Camping and exploring new places is FUN, and being prepared is the best way to make sure it stays fun! Have fun!

Made in the USA
San Bernardino, CA
16 July 2017